# Being a Man After God's Own Heart

*Always take time to reflect*

*Daniel*

## David Dayler

**NOVALIS**

© 2013 Novalis Publishing Inc.

Cover design: Blaine Herrmann
Cover image: Jupiter Images
Layout: Audrey Wells

Published by Novalis

Publishing Office
10 Lower Spadina Avenue, Suite 400
Toronto, Ontario, Canada
M5V 2Z2

Head Office
4475 Frontenac Street
Montréal, Québec, Canada
H2H 2S2
www.novalis.ca

Library and Archives Canada Cataloguing in Publication

Dayler, David, 1949-
    Being a man after God's own heart / David Dayler.

Issued also in an electronic format. ISBN 978-2-89646-489-0

    1. Catholic men--Religious life.  2. Catholic men--Prayers and devotions.
3. Catholic men--Biography. I. Title.

BX2352.5.D39 2013          248.8>42          C2013-901658-9

Printed in Canada.

The Scripture quotations contained herein are from the New Revised Standard Version of the Bible, copyrighted 1989 by the Division of Christian Education of the National Council of the Churches of Christ in the United States of America, and are used by permission. All rights reserved.

We acknowledge the financial support of the Government of Canada through the Canada Book Fund for business development activities.

5  4  3  2  1          17    16    15    14    13

*As for you, man of God ... pursue righteousness, godliness, faith, love, endurance, gentleness.*

1 Timothy 6:11

I dedicate this book to
Linda, Matthew, Nathan, and Zachary –
the ones who continually teach me
the most profound lessons of love and faith.

# Table of Contents

*Reflecting on our personal faith journey*
*through the lives of fifteen men of faith*

# Foreword

"A few good men" – fifteen, in fact – is what this book is all about. Not only does David Dayler provide information about each of the men he presents, but he also tells us what makes them "good." And more, he reflects with us how, by following their examples, we, too, might be good!

The men we read about in this book are not perfect – goodness is not about being perfect – but when all is said and done, they are faithful, and they are made good by God's grace at work in them.

This is a book for men: men who want to know what goodness means, men who desire goodness, men who are ready to make the commitment to seek it in their lives. If you are already perfect, you don't need this book. If you are still on the journey, this book will be a helpful read.

Because the author presents so many different examples of good men, the reader will surely find one or two or more to whom he will relate more easily – men who have recognized and accepted their weaknesses and who, in doing so, have given themselves over completely to a loving God!

Reading *Being a Man after God's Own Heart* is like going on a good retreat. Read it on a quiet Sunday afternoon, or read it a chapter at a time, reflecting on the questions provided at the end of each story – however you choose to read it, you will be changed!

Men who are members of the Knights of Columbus will find this book particularly interesting. The final insightful chapter is dedicated to the life of Father Michael McGivney, the inspired founder of that order.

By writing this book, David Dayler has given men a gift. He reminds us that God calls us all to holiness, and he shows us just how remarkable that call is for any man who dares to open his heart to God.

*Bishop Douglas Crosby, OMI*
*Bishop of Hamilton*
*August 24, 2012*

# Preface

The world today is a fast-paced, technologically driven, multi-faceted one – a world in which many find that the busyness of life hampers our relationship with God. We spend so much time addressing the activities of day-to-day living that we forget the importance of building and nurturing our spiritual lives through personal prayer and reflection. Let's face it; we live in a world of distractions, a world that makes it very hard for us to hear God's voice.

Today, as Catholic men, we assume many and varied roles in our daily lives. We are sons, husbands, fathers and colleagues. Each role requires different skill sets and presents its own challenges. How do we balance these many and varied roles? How do we find time to be with God?

Being a man after God's own heart may seem like an unattainable goal for modern men. How can we, as St. Paul tells us, "Rejoice always, pray without ceasing, give thanks in all circumstances; for this is the will of God in Christ Jesus for you" (1 Thessalonians 5:16-18)?

As a basic Christian message, this is not bad advice. Prayer must be a part of our daily lives. It is through prayer that our priorities begin to change and our focus moves towards our relationship with God. Whether as a married man, a single man, or an ordained priest, a Catholic man needs to listen, to pray and to test the waters in order to discover the plan that God has for him. God is looking for "a few good men"! Where does God turn? It is not always to the most saintly, the most pious, the most holy. God turns to us all.

When I began writing this book of reflections, I based it on two verses of scripture that have always drawn me to deeper reflection. In 1 Samuel 13:14, King Saul is admonished, "but now your kingdom will not continue; the Lord has sought out a man after his own heart"; and then in 1 Samuel 16:7 we hear, "for the Lord does not see as mortals see; they look on the outward appearance, but the Lord looks on the heart."

We tend to forget that we cannot apply our contemporary understandings of time and reason to God's work. God does not work according to our schedule, our timeline, but in God's own time. God does not see as we see; as the scripture tells us, God looks "on the heart." From these verses of scripture came the title for this book: *Being a Man after God's Own Heart.*

When I sat with the stories of the men featured in this book, I was constantly reminded of the above verses from the First Book of Samuel. Here were men, mostly ordinary men, with countless human failings and weaknesses, and yet each, in his own way, served God. God saw beyond their human frailties into their very hearts and found willing participants in his plan. As I spent time with the stories of the lives of these fifteen ordinary men called to do God's work, I knew that each of them had a message for us today: that each of these men could help us see how modern men might deepen our personal relationship with God and in turn might become more receptive, more open to God's call to service.

It is my hope that as you reflect on these stories and the lives of these men, you will be able to make connections to your personal faith journey and be open to hearing what the Lord has in store for you. These stories are not meant to stand alone, but to be read and reflected upon in light of your daily life. The messages found within them will speak in a different way to each reader, as he brings his own faith and experience to the stories.

Just as these fifteen men are models for approaching how we live our lives today, they remind us that we have a responsibility to interpret their core messages and apply them within our daily context. Whatever age or stage we are at, God is calling us – not necessarily to change the world, but to help build God's kingdom of love through our actions and our deeds at home, at work and in our faith communities. The stories in this book help show us that all men, regardless of the challenges they face, have the potential to be men after God's own heart.

Early in my faith journey, I struggled along a rocky path. My mother was a member of the United Church and my father was Presbyterian; as a family, we attended the United Church regularly, but there wasn't much depth to my faith. As I grew older, I was searching, but I wasn't sure what I was searching for. There was an emptiness that I couldn't explain. Gradually, my personal relationship with God seemed to weaken and falter. Then I met my wife, Linda, a cradle Catholic, and around the same time I got to know a priest who eventually became not only my mentor, but a lifelong friend. Through study and prayer, I discovered the power and beauty of the Catholic faith. My relationship with God grew stronger and more dynamic. God graciously welcomed me back, and my life has been a great adventure ever since! The rocks are still there, but God is there to help me climb them. God, in his great mercy, will do this for anyone – young or old – who approaches him. By immersing ourselves in these stories of men of our faith tradition, we can see that God wants all of us, with all our imperfections, to be men after God's own heart.

Throughout history, God has called ordinary men to do extraordinary things! I hope that you – whether on your own or as part of a men's group – will use this book as a springboard for discussion and personal reflection. I invite you to sit with these stories and use the reflection questions provided to further explore your call to be a man after God's own heart.

The men in this book were all flawed beings who answered God's call. Today, in our brokenness and humanity, we turn to them as models and guides for our journey: a journey that draws us closer to God and sends us forth to help bring about God's kingdom here and now.

Here is our prayer as we begin:

## LET US PRAY +

Gracious God,
as we begin our reflections
on being a man after your own heart,
we are reminded that you walk with us always
on our journey of discovery.
We remember that you call us,
even in our brokenness,
to be men of faith.
We pray that through the guidance of the Holy Spirit,
we may fully realize our potential as Catholic men.
We ask this through Christ our Lord.
Amen. +

# Men of the Old Testament

# Abraham

*Being a man of trust*

*Did you not, O our God, drive out the inhabitants of this land before your people Israel, and give it forever to the descendants of your friend Abraham?*

2 Chronicles 20:7

Today the words "obedience" and "trust" are often under siege, as nations fight for democracy rather than accepting a tyrant leader and investment companies go bankrupt overnight, taking people's life savings with them. Yet most of us obey the rules of the road when we drive and follow the laws of the land when it comes to our business dealings. Despite the occasional disappointment or betrayal, we trust that we will be treated fairly in all we do. We seem to do so with little thought – over time, it has become a habit. We know the laws and so we follow them. In our reflection on Abraham, we explore the place that obedience and trust have in our faith lives. Here, "obedience" means complying with someone's wishes or orders, while "trust" reflects a firm reliance on God's care.

Abraham, our ancestor in faith, is considered the father of God's people. What was there about Abraham that God singled him out to be the father of nations?

Abraham lived in the city of Ur with his wife, Sarah. One day the Lord said to Abraham, "Go from your country and your kindred and your father's house to the land that I will show you. I will make of you a great nation, and I will bless you, and make your name great, so that you will be a blessing. I will bless those who bless you, and the one who curses you I will curse; and in you all the families of the earth shall be blessed" (Genesis 12:1-3). What God was asking of Abraham was no small task. He was to uproot himself from all that he knew and loved and set off on a journey based purely on obedience and faith.

The covenant or promise that God made with Abraham was this: Abraham would become the father of a nation from which would come the Saviour of the world. (For a more complete look at the covenant between God and Abraham, read Genesis 17:1-8.) By keeping this covenant, Abraham would be greatly blessed.

This covenant with God is not unlike the contracts we enter into today, such as for a loan, a mortgage, a business partnership or a marriage. Each partner agrees to specific terms. Abram was to obey God and live a blameless life. God would bless Abraham with many children and they in turn would produce many nations.

Indeed, faith and obedience are the hallmarks of Abraham's life. He loved God deeply and showed his love through faith and obedience. While Abraham's faith is an example for us all, we are called to model his obedience in our lives as well. How can we show our obedience to God today? The covenantal relationship is a good place to begin. God always upholds his part of the covenant – we are called to be his people and he will be our God. For our part, we need to obey his teachings. We are called to trust in these – whether it be by living the teachings of the Ten Commandments or living the way of the Beatitudes – not simply to obey rules or laws, but to trust in their truths and to live them fully. Abraham trusted God completely, as we discover throughout his story in Genesis. He trusted God to provide. In this reflection, we focus on the story of Abraham being asked to sacrifice his son Isaac, for it truly exemplifies Abraham's limitless trust.

When God formed his covenant with Abraham, Abraham was already 99 years old – not exactly the ideal age at which to begin a family. We are amazed to hear of the birth of Isaac (after all, Sarah herself was 90!). Then we are shocked to read that God is asking Abraham to sacrifice their only son (Genesis 22:1-18). What must have gone through Abraham's mind when God told him to take his young son to the mountain and to offer him as a sacrifice to God? He must have been torn between his love for his beloved child and his desire to obey his God. The power in this story is not the shock value of a man asked to sacrifice his son, but Abraham's trust and obedience in God's plan. The key to Abraham's faith was his trust in God; because of his faith, he could be completely obedient to God's call.

We, too, are called to have faith like Abraham's. We are called to have a faith that is transformative – that transforms lives. Abraham was ready to do anything and everything that God asked of him. In Abraham's mind, nothing was impossible with God on his side. God would provide. Time and time again, God tested Abraham's faith. It wasn't always easy for Abraham – like many of us, he was weak, impatient and fearful, and was known to lie under pressure. All of these traits come to the fore when Abraham and Sarah are in Egypt. Abraham lies about his relationship with Sarah, introducing her as his sister because he knows his life would be in danger if Pharaoh knew that this beautiful woman was his wife; as her brother, he would be protected and honoured. Through God's intervention, the covenant relationship was maintained and Abraham was forgiven. Clearly, God can and will use us in spite of our weaknesses.

What is the role of obedience in our lives as Catholic men? In today's world, *disobedience* seems to be the cultural norm. People the world over are rebelling against all forms of authority, whether in government, society or the Church. Yet as Catholics, we are all called to obey God, just as Abraham did.

When we put the word of God into practice in our daily lives, God will bless us as he did Abraham. God is seeking the humbleness of obedience and faith within our hearts.

Abraham was blessed by God through his faith. He was obedient to God, but it was his faith that allowed him to be obedient. We can pray for humble, open minds so that we can draw closer to God not only through our actions but through our total commitment to and trust in God.

# Reflection Questions

*Abraham put his ultimate trust in God and was fiercely obedient to God's will.*

1. How well do you follow the rules of the road, regulations in your workplace and society's laws? How attentive or obedient are you to the call to be faithful to God? How can you become more faithful?

2. Giving up control can be especially difficult for men. Think about a time when you had to let others – your spouse, son or daughter, for example – follow their own path. What did it take for you to accept that you were not going to be in charge of the situation?

3. Placing ultimate trust and faith in God's plan was not easy for Abraham. Reflect on a time in your life when it was difficult to accept or follow God's plan for you. Who helped you through this challenging time?

# LET US PRAY +

Heavenly Father,
as Abraham placed his trust in you
and offered unconditional obedience,
we ask that through your support
and the nurturing of the Holy Spirit,
we, like Abraham, with great humility,
will open our minds,
place our full trust in you,
and always obey your will for us.
We ask this through Christ our Lord.
Amen. +

# David

*Being a man to whom much is given,*
*and therefore much is required*

*I have found David, son of Jesse, to be a man after my heart, who*
*will carry out all my wishes.*

Acts 13:22

*Make me to know your ways, O Lord;*
*teach me your paths.*
*Lead me in your truth, and teach me,*
*for you are the God of my salvation;*
*for you I wait all day long.*

Psalm 25:4-5

If David can be a man after God's own heart, there is hope for us all! As the youngest of Jesse's eight sons, David was a man of many talents. One of the best-known and beloved figures of the Old Testament, David was a shepherd, a mighty warrior, a gifted musician and a king. His great weakness and downfall was that he was a ladies' man. In 1 and 2 Samuel,

1 Kings and 1 Chronicles we meet David, but the Psalms reveal to us the heart of David.

It is in certain Psalms, many of which have been attributed to him, that we see the outpouring of David's soul and his dependence on God. This is not the dependence of someone who cannot make decisions or take action, but a dependence on God for guidance in making these decisions.

As a young boy, David challenged the Philistines' champion, Goliath, when no other man would. "What shall be done for the man who kills this Philistine, and takes away the reproach from Israel?" he demanded. "For who is this uncircumcised Philistine, that he should defy the armies of the living God?" (1 Samuel 17:26). What followed has become legend: David, by putting his trust in God, was able to defeat Goliath. This story of the young shepherd defeating the enormous, powerful Goliath has become a metaphor for us today as we find the strength to stand up to our greatest challenges, knowing that by placing all our trust in God we can succeed. Too often we think that we have to do everything on our own – that we are totally responsible for all that happens, turning to God only in times of crisis. Like David, we need to acknowledge, honour and reverence God with our whole heart, not just as an outward expression but with our entire being. Honouring and obeying God must be the first steps we take, not a last resort.

David rose from the lonely life of a shepherd to being one of Israel's most renowned kings. Did David sit around reading the scriptures and meditating all day? We know for a fact that he didn't! Nor was David perfect: he sinned and made mistakes. He was much like us; although he had faith in God and placed his trust in him, there were times when he lacked faith. Yet, despite his failings, God called him a man after his own heart.

As a warrior, David shed much blood (1 Chronicles 22:8); he was a neglectful father, and his family suffered as a result (2 Samuel 13:15-18, 28-29; 18:33); he went against God's command and out of pride counted the number of his troops, which resulted in seventy thousand of his people dying in a plague (2 Samuel 24:10-15).

He also committed adultery (2 Samuel 11). From the palace rooftop, David observed Bathsheba bathing. Captivated by her beauty, he sent for her. Although she was married to Uriah the Hittite, Bathsheba had no choice but to go. David was, after all, the king. David committed adultery with Bathsheba and she became pregnant. In order to cover up his sin, David tried to get Uriah to return home to be with his wife so that people might think the child was Uriah's. When all his efforts failed, David had Uriah sent to the front lines in battle, where he was killed.

Later, God sent the prophet Nathan to confront David with this sin. Many people, when faced with their sins, deny any responsibility, or they blame others. But David said to Nathan, "I have sinned against the Lord" (2 Samuel 12:13). David confessed his sin with a contrite heart. We, too, must accept responsibility for our weaknesses and for giving in to temptation.

God allowed David to rise to great heights and sink into the depths of sin. Yet God knew the depth of David's love for him.

God's love for David overcame the bad: "The Lord does not see as mortals see; they look on the outward appearance, but the Lord looks on the heart" (1 Samuel 16:7). God will do the same for us if we let him in.

Does this mean we can live our lives any way we want, justifying everything with the thought that God will forgive us as long as we are sorry? No. The story of David shows us that as men of intellect, will and spirit, we must exercise control over desires that cause us to reject or overlook what we know is right and just. Our society today often seeks instant gratification and pleasure; it is not so different from David's world. We, like David, constantly struggle with what we want to do, what we should do, and what we are called to do.

It is very popular today to blame our sins on issues from our past: our parents, our employers, or hardships we have had to endure. We easily shift the responsibility away from ourselves onto the actions of others. Yet in the end, we are accountable for our actions and our responsibilities before God. David had his faults, but he was willing to do whatever God asked him to do. "I have found David, son of Jesse, to be a man after my heart, who will carry out my wishes" (Acts 13:22). He will carry out my wishes! Can we say the same? How simple it sounds, and yet how hard for us to imitate.

As we see in the scriptures, David's life involved bloodshed, personal sin and difficult times. What makes David stand out is not these experiences but his response to them. His approach leaves us with the impression of a man who was truly committed to God. By his actions, it is obvious that David didn't deserve God's blessings. But within his heart David had the right desire. Ultimately, he wanted to please God. David prayed for everything – not just in crisis, but for everything. We see this clearly in the Psalms, where he pours out his heart and avows his trust in God, and gives thanks for God's goodness and mercy, power and justice for all. David's words in the Psalms reflect a broad variety of life issues in the life of both the individual and the nation as a whole.

If you are like me, you have a tendency to take three steps forward and two steps back in your spiritual walk with God. When that happens, remember David and how he kept his sights on God, even in difficult moments.

## Reflection Questions

*God wants an eternal relationship with us. We don't even have to make the first move; his hand is outstretched, waiting for us to take hold. What is keeping you from spending more time developing your relationship with God?*

1. Despite David's brokenness and failings, when God looked into David's heart, he found the man he was looking for. What does God see when he looks into your heart?

2. While many of life's daily activities chained David to the secular world, the desires of his heart always led

him back to the Lord. We often get so wrapped up in our troubles, despair, depression, suffering and sorrows that we forget that God protects us and delivers us from the chains that bind. What are some of the "chains" that bind you to your secular life and keep you from spending time developing your relationship with God? In other words, what is keeping you from opening your heart to God?

3. Speaking of chains, reflect for a few minutes on envy and pride – two of the "deadly sins" of the Christian tradition. David's story reminds us at times of both these failings. Think of a moment in your life when they got in the way of your faith life as well as your human relationships. What did you do? Would you do things differently now?

4. Can you think of a time in your life when, like David, you drifted away from God? What brought you back?

5. How often do you pray in moments of crisis and trouble but forget to pray in thanksgiving for a beautiful day, time with family, or a chance encounter with an old friend? How can you remember to pray in all circumstances?

# LET US PRAY +

Heavenly Father,
your love for David saw beyond
the human failings of the man
to see the inner workings of his heart.
Through prayer and reflection,
David grew in his love for you.
Grant that we may grow in our prayer life
and strengthen our commitment to you,
so that we too may heed your call to action.
We ask this through Christ our Lord.
Amen. +

# Job

**_Being a man who perseveres through great suffering_**

_Then Job arose, tore his robe, shaved his head, and fell on the ground and worshipped. He said, "Naked I came from my mother's womb, and naked shall I return there; the Lord gave, and the Lord has taken away; blessed be the name of the Lord."_

_In all this Job did not sin or charge God with wrongdoing._

Job 1:20-22

W hy do bad things happen to good people? How often have you asked yourself that question? How often has someone said to you, "How can God let this happen?"

The Book of Job and Job himself remind us that even the just may suffer and that their suffering is a test of their fidelity. The Book of Job is a "must read" dramatic poem that explores the problem of the suffering of the innocent, and of retribution. I encourage you to take the time to read the entire book of Job. For now, I will tell you what you need to know about this biblical character.

Job was a wealthy man, happy in his home and family, until his good fortune was completely reversed. This father of seven sons and three daughters lived with his wife in Uz. He was blessed with much land and abundant livestock, and lived his life loving God and worshipping him daily. Then Job lost everything as a result of Satan's intervention. When God said, "There is no one like him on the earth, a blameless and upright man who fears God and turns away from evil" (Job 1:8), Satan replied, "Does Job fear God for nothing? Have you not put a fence around him and his house and all that he has, on every side? You have blessed the work of his hands, and his possessions have increased in the land. But stretch out your hand now, and touch all that he has, and he will curse you to your face" (Job 1:9-11).

And so it began. God gave Satan the power to test Job. "Very well, all that he has is in your power; only do not stretch out your hand against him!" (Job 1:12).

Despite all that befell him, Job would not turn his back on God. When his wife criticized him for not reacting to the hardships they were facing, he replied, "You speak as any foolish woman would speak. Shall we receive the good at the hand of God, and not receive the bad?" (Job 2:10). Job truly is a model of a man after God's own heart. He is often called the great sufferer. He offers us a portrait by which we can and should measure ourselves.

Job took great delight in, and was blessed with, his children. He was devoted to them and prayed for them constantly. When he was informed of their deaths, the heartache was beyond belief, and yet he "fell on the ground and worshipped" (Job 1:20). Knowing that God was in control, and that his children were given by God and ultimately taken by God, he could worship.

Job's friends were certain that God was punishing Job for some unrevealed sin. Job adamantly denied any such sin and maintained his respect for and obedience to God. However, as is the case for many of us, during his ordeal and time of trial, Job came to resent God.

We often think of Job in terms of his trial of faith and the challenges and afflictions of his life. We hear much about his suffering and pain. What is often overlooked is the result: in the end, because of the qualities of his character, he is victorious and is redeemed.

What were these qualities that got him through this tremendous struggle? What strength of character did he need to face almost unimaginable pain? Throughout his struggles, Job never forgot God, and never forgot that God cared for him no matter how much Job suffered. "Oh, that I were as in the months of old, as in the days when God watched over me; when his lamp shone over my head, and by his light I walked through darkness" (Job 29:2-3). A man after God's own heart never forgets God. In good times and in bad, and especially in times of great trial, being mindful of God's presence sustains us.

In the end, Job saw that the root of his problem was his lack of understanding and his over-confidence in his own righteousness: "I have uttered what I did not understand, things too wonderful for me, which I did not know. Hear, and I will speak;

I will question you, and you declare to me. I had heard of you by the hearing of the ear, but now my eye sees you; therefore I despise myself, and repent in dust and ashes" (Job 42:3-6).

Just as Job gradually came to resent God amid his suffering, we also may turn away in resentment and say, "Why me?" when we are facing great challenges. We may feel that God is not responding to us and not acknowledging our fidelity and righteousness. Like Job, we must look honestly at our own actions and attitudes: we may lack understanding and be too sure of our own righteousness. From Job's story we can learn the danger of holding ourselves in too high esteem. Like Job, we forget that God sees and knows far more than we ever could.

We must never assume that God isn't listening or simply doesn't care. Even within the midst of our suffering, we must put our trust in God. Many people today tend to walk away from God when they are faced with turmoil and struggle. Job reminds us that living our lives and our faith is a challenge, but one that a man after God's own heart is willing to meet head on.

# Reflection Questions

*God always listens to us and cares for us. No matter how severe the trial or the challenge, God sees beyond the present moment and our faulty understanding, guiding us in the lessons we need to learn.*

*As Catholic men seeking to be men after God's own heart, we can learn from Job's experiences by maintaining patient respect and ultimate trust in God, even in moments of deep suffering and despair.*

1. Have you experienced moments of great loss, such as those faced by Job? Could you see God in these experiences, or not? How did your relationship with God change as a result?

2. Have there been times of great turmoil when you questioned the presence of God? How did you resolve this questioning?

3. As men, we tend to feel we must be strong and hold everyone together. Who holds you together in times of great stress? Does your faith in God help you through these times of need? How?

# LET US PRAY +

Gracious God,
grant us the strength of Job as we face
the challenges of our lives.
Give us patience when people try to draw us
away from you.
Guide and protect us when we are struggling,
and help us remember that
we do not face our trials alone,
and that through your constant loving presence
we will persevere.
We ask this through Christ our Lord.
Amen. +

# Daniel

## *Being a man of deep conviction*

*"Dare to be a Daniel.
Dare to stand alone!
Dare to have a purpose firm!
Dare to make it known!"*

"Dare to Be a Daniel," by Philip P. Bliss

The story of the prophet Daniel challenges us to not be afraid to stand firm in our faith. The words of the hymn above, written in 1873 by Philip P. Bliss, encourage us to dare as Daniel did – dare to stand; dare to have a purpose; dare to make that purpose known! Daniel, one of the great figures of the Old Testament, rose to a position of high authority in a foreign land amidst great adversity. His life spanned the entire time of the Jewish captivity in Babylon.

Even as a young man, Daniel was a person of deep conviction. He had been raised as a Jew and loved God deeply. He was among the first group of Hebrews to be deported in 605 B.C., when King Nebuchadnezzar laid siege to the city of Judah.

The king chose Daniel to be part of his court, as he met certain criteria: "young men without physical defect and handsome, versed in every branch of wisdom, endowed with knowledge and insight, and competent to serve in the king's palace" (Daniel 1:4). From the very beginning, Daniel decided in his heart that he would not allow this situation to cause him to defile himself or turn away from his God. Many scholars believe that as part of being brought into the court, Daniel became a eunuch (was castrated), and yet he remained firm in his faith. In this new land and in the king's court, Daniel served under three kings during his lifetime. He was exposed to the wealth and luxury of Babylon and became well versed in the language, literature and culture, but refused to be seduced by the allure of all that was presented to him, and remained consecrated to God.

Imagine how Daniel must have felt: separated from family and those he loved, a stranger in a strange land, a slave in the king's court. He knew he was in an impossible situation from which he could not escape. All he could do was maintain his sense of integrity, honour and devotion to his God.

Because the food and drink in the court were unclean for Jews, he "resolved that he would not defile himself with the royal rations of food and wine; so he asked the palace master to allow him not to defile himself" (Daniel 1:8). He had more respect for and fear of God than he did for the Babylonian kings.

Trusting that God had a plan for him, he kept his mind focused on God. Still, Daniel found much favour in the eyes of the Babylonian kings and was given great power. With great power, however, came those who wanted to see him fall from grace. Out of jealousy and mistrust, they looked for ways to discredit him.

They convinced King Darius to "establish an ordinance and enforce an interdict, that whoever prays to anyone, divine or human, for thirty days, except to you, O king, shall be thrown into a den of lions" (Daniel 6:7). When Daniel learned of this, he was undeterred; he continued with his prayer life. "Although Daniel knew that the document had been signed, he continued to go to his house, which had windows in its upper room open toward Jerusalem, and to get down on his knees three times a day to pray to his God and praise him, just as he had done previously" (Daniel 6:10). Here we see one of Daniel's greatest gifts: the gift of prayer. All great men of God are men of prayer, and Daniel was no exception. His conversation with God – for that is what prayer is – was of the utmost importance to him. It sustained him and kept him connected to God.

Daniel prayed even when he was told not to. When his detractors confronted him, Daniel was willingly brought before King Darius. As a result of his decree, which by tradition could not be altered once it had been made, Darius had no choice but to throw Daniel into the lions' den. The king, who loved and respected David, was deeply upset. The morning after Daniel was thrown to the lions, Darius returned to the sealed den and in a distressed voice called, "O Daniel, servant of the living God, has your God whom you faithfully serve been able to deliver you from the lions?" (Daniel 6:19). Daniel replied, "O king, live forever! My God sent his angel and shut the lions' mouths so that they would not hurt me, because I was found blameless before him; and also before you, O king, I have done no wrong" (Daniel 6:21-22). The king was overjoyed. Darius had Daniel pulled from the den and released, and had his accusers brought down and thrown into the lions' den along with their wives and families. In response to what he had witnessed, King Darius said, "I make a decree, that in all my royal dominion people should tremble and fear before the God of Daniel: For he is the living God, enduring forever. His kingdom shall never be destroyed, and his dominion has no end. He delivers and rescues, he works signs and wonders in heaven and on earth; for he has saved Daniel from the power of the lions" (Daniel 6:26-27).

So many of us today forget that God has a plan for us as we forge ahead with our own plans without stopping to consider where God might be guiding us. Daniel accepted being thrown to the lions rather than offend God.

From Daniel we learn that we must always do what is right, regardless of the cost. Sometimes it is much easier to do wrong than right, and often more pleasing. But just as with Daniel, we can be assured that God's love will give us courage. If we, like Daniel, have the courage to do what is right, the "lions" we face today cannot destroy us. We will be safe in the love of God. Like Daniel, we live in a world where moral darkness and secular influences challenge our relationship with God. Today's "lions" may be less obvious than Daniel's but are just as effective at forcing us to abandon our principles. Social issues, from the dignity of human life to a growing lack of interest in organized religion, are but a few of the challenges to our faith we face as Catholic men today. We are confronted by them in our offices and on our factory floors; in our mass media, schools and legislatures; even in our sports arenas. They often carry the power of conventional wisdom – and by defying it we appear foolish or old-fashioned. Today's lion's den can be the talk radio shows, letters to the editor in the daily newspaper, the blogosphere, even the lunchroom gatherings in our workplaces – and it is words instead of teeth that wound us.

As we reflect on the story of Daniel, we are reminded of the courage that Daniel showed in staying faithful to God in the midst of life-threatening persecution. This faithful man was able to find hope even within a seemingly hopeless situation. He found comfort and strength in his prayer to God.

We, too, may find ourselves confused and at times afraid to engage in the death-dealing issues of today's world. As models of faith for our families, friends and co-workers, however, we must find the courage to stand firm and trust in God. Like Daniel, we must be men of prayer, open and willing to stand up and face the "lions" in our lives and in the lives of our families. As we deepen our prayer life, we become men of prayer, men of God, men of faith.

## Reflection Questions

*"Dare to be a Daniel, dare to stand alone!"*

1. What defiles your relationship with God today? Name a few examples from your life. →

2. How can you separate yourself from the things that would defile you? Where can you find the courage to do so?

3. What "lions" do you find yourself facing? How do you react in these situations? If you find these moments difficult, how can you find new ways of responding? How can you arm yourself – psychologically, intellectually and spiritually – to deal with these challenges?

4. Daniel found courage and strength in prayer. What does prayer offer you?

## LET US PRAY +

Heavenly Father,
Daniel stood strong and firm and dedicated his life to you.
He never allowed anything to defile
his relationship with his God.
In the midst of the challenges we face today,
in a world filled with secular temptations,
we ask for the strength to offer our lives
to your greater glory.
We ask this through Christ our Lord.
Amen. +

# Jacob

*Being a man who struggles with his faith*

*"You shall no longer be called Jacob, but Israel, for you have
striven with God and with humans, and have prevailed."*

Genesis 32:28

J acob's story is a powerful example of transformation
and conversion. What can we learn from him? At times
we may have more in common with him than we care
to acknowledge.

Jacob's early life was filled with deception. After Abraham's
death, God revealed to Abraham's son Isaac that he would be
the father of two sons who would represent two nations. Isaac's
wife, Rebekah, gave birth to twin boys. Esau, who was born first,
was extremely hairy. Jacob, whose skin was smooth, was born
second, holding his brother's heel. These two brothers grew to be
polar opposites of one another. Jacob was soft spoken but quick
witted, while Esau was brash and not as bright. Jacob managed
to steal Esau's inheritance in exchange for a bowl of food that
Jacob provided when Esau was hungry (Genesis 25:29-34). This
was Jacob's first deception, but not his last!

Much later in life, when their father, who was blind, was near death, Isaac told Esau, who was a hunter, to prepare and serve him a meal so that he might give Esau his blessing. While Esau was out hunting game for the meal, Jacob, with his mother's help, prepared a separate meal. Then Jacob, wearing a hairy skin so his skin would feel like Esau's, presented the meal to his father. Believing Jacob to be Esau, Isaac imparted his blessing on Jacob, promising him the inheritance of God's covenant and much greater status than his brother.

This hardly seems like the making of a man after God's own heart, but read on! Following this deception, Jacob, fearing Esau's reaction to what had happened, fled to his uncle Laban's home in Mesopotamia. On this journey, he had a dream of a stairway leading up to heaven. In the dream, God promised him the same covenant that God had made with Abraham and Isaac. "Then Jacob made a vow, saying, 'If God will be with me, and will keep me in this way that I go, and will give me bread to eat and clothing to wear, so that I come again to my father's house in peace, then the Lord shall be my God, and this stone, which I have set up for a pillar, shall be God's house; and of all that you give me I will surely give one tenth to you'" (Genesis 28:20-22). After the dream, he wanted to pay back God for all he had been given. So he rose early in the morning, took the stone that he had put under his head and used it as a pillar. He poured oil on top of it and called that place Bethel, a place where people could worship God. Following this transformative experience, Jacob submitted the rest of his life to God. Through this encounter with God, Jacob became humble before the Lord.

Upon his arrival at the home of Laban, Jacob offered to work for his uncle in exchange for the hand of Laban's daughter Rachel. This time, however, it was Jacob who was deceived. He was tricked into marrying the older daughter, Leah, before being allowed to marry Rachel.

Years later, after a stormy family life in Mesopotamia, Jacob returned home to make amends with Esau. On this journey he spent the night alone on the banks of the River Jabbok at Peniel. Here he met a stranger, God disguised as a man, who physically wrestled with Jacob until dawn. After a night of great struggle, Jacob demanded a blessing from his opponent. The man blessed Jacob by renaming him "Israel," meaning "he struggles with God" (Genesis 32:22-30).

In that night of struggle on the banks of the River Jabbok, the story of Jacob speaks to us as Catholic men today. We can probably see something of ourselves in him. He was not a perfect man; he had many character flaws. He constantly tried to get the best of others if he could, yet God's grace transformed him. This transformation or conversion was not swift or painless. As we see from Jacob's years of struggle and encounters with God, the transformative experience can be lonely and painful. Today, we often are looking for quick responses to our questions when what we should be looking for is insight, for insight leads us to transformation and conversion. Our transformation will in turn lead to a change in priorities within our lives that will allow our relationship with God to grow and deepen. Through this transformation, we will find that prayer will play a more significant role in our lives, and we will find it easier to reject the allure of those things that can damage our personal relationship with God.

The New Testament offers us a connection to the Old Testament story of Jacob: "So [God's mercy and compassion] depend not on human will or exertion, but on God who shows mercy" (Romans 9:16). God wants to transform us, but we must be willing. The Gospel of Matthew says, "But strive first for the kingdom of God and his righteousness, and all these things will be given to you as well" (6:33).

This lonely, painful transformative experience is best seen in Jacob's struggle on the banks of the Jabbok River at Peniel. It is here that Jacob both literally and figuratively wrestles with God. After struggling with God, who is disguised as a man, at Peniel, Jacob becomes a changed man. At the end of his life, years later in Egypt, he is a respected man of wisdom. Although he had been a man of great deception, he changed when his heart focused on what God had promised.

The image of wrestling is easy for us to understand. Conflict, struggle and confusion are all part of the process when we wrestle with difficult issues. In relationships, when both parties are in sync and working together, we often say they are "dancing to the same tune," and so it is with God. At times we wrestle and struggle, resisting the transformative experiences; at other times, we are in sync, in harmony. Whether we wrestle or dance with God, we can be led to transformation.

For we are all called to transformation: no matter what struggles and challenges we face, no matter the state of our lives, we can always be transformed by God's grace as long as we are open to the call. Transformation does not mean the end of suffering or challenges – in Jacob's case, his sons became deceivers and murders, his daughter was disgraced (Genesis 34); he lost his favourite son, Joseph (Genesis 37) and was separated for a long time from his youngest child, Benjamin (Genesis 43) – but a renewed relationship with God gives us the strength to deal with whatever life throws at us.

Pope Benedict, in his weekly audience on May 25, 2011, expanded on the story of Jacob and how it speaks to us today. The pope stressed that we can truly encounter God through humility and perseverance in prayer. He added, "God's blessing cannot be won by force but rather must be received with humility from God himself." Speaking directly of the struggle between Jacob and God at the riverbank, he said that during the struggle, when Jacob seemed to be winning, Jacob demanded that his opponent bless him. The man turned the tables by asking Jacob his name – which at that time was a very probing question, for a person's name was their very identity. The challenger (God) gave Jacob the name "Israel" – which gave him a new and honest identity.

Like Jacob, we all experience from time to time what St. John of the Cross called the "dark night of the soul" – our struggle for illumination. In this painful process, we must face our weaknesses and failings. Yet through prayer, reflection and trust in God, we can, as Jacob did, emerge from the process renewed in our relationship with God. And it is never too late.

# Reflection Questions

*Humility and perseverance in prayer is rewarded by a true encounter with God.*

Pope Benedict XVI, General Audience, May 25, 2011

1. Like Jacob, our relationship with God may seem complicated and even volatile. At times we struggle with God; at times we dance with God. Think about those moments in your life when you felt the struggle. How did those moments affect your relationship with God?

2. Despite numerous setbacks and moments when Jacob gave in to his weaknesses, he always returned to God. And God was there waiting for him. How might our own pride, stubbornness or fear prevent us from turning to God?

3. Through dance, we work collaboratively with a partner to explore the music. When you dance with God and allow the music of God's Word to fill your soul, you will find yourself becoming more open to hear his call. Reflect on those moments when you felt you have truly danced with God. If these moments are few and far between, think about how you can become more open to God's voice in your life.

# LET US PRAY +

Gracious God,
just as Jacob wrestled with his doubts and fears,
we, too, wrestle at times with the choices we make.
We ask for your patience and perseverance
in allowing us to struggle,
knowing that this struggle will lead us
into a deeper relationship with you.
We ask this through Christ our Lord.
Amen. +

# Men of the New Testament

# St. Joseph

## Being a man who is just

*What emanates from the figure of St. Joseph is faith...*
*Joseph of Nazareth is a "just man"*
*because he totally "lives by faith."*
*He is holy because his faith is truly heroic.*

Blessed Pope John Paul II

So often we have heard that God calls ordinary men to do extraordinary things. Not everyone called to do God's work has led an unblemished life. In fact, we need only look at most of the biblical figures explored in this book to see that each and every one of them faced struggles, challenges, doubts and fears. While many called by God were considered movers and shakers within their communities, many more were ordinary men like you and me.

No greater example of an ordinary man can be found than Joseph of Nazareth. No prophet, poet or king, Joseph led the life of a simple carpenter. His life and livelihood may have been simple, but there was nothing simple about his faith. How can we be so sure of this when we know so little about Joseph? Because of his *actions* and his response to God's call. Each time God called, Joseph complied, immediately and completely. He asked no questions and didn't argue. Without a single word, he responded. He didn't need to speak to God for clarification, as he was in complete communion with God through prayer and through his faith and trust in what God was asking him to do. This was enough for Joseph! That is why some people call him the silent steward of the Word.

Many of us today say we don't know where to start when it comes to prayer. We feel we don't know how to speak to God. We have no words to express our thoughts. Turning to St. Joseph may help.

For in our world that is constantly seeking role models for motherhood and fatherhood, Joseph is well worth emulating. If we are to model ourselves after St. Joseph, let us begin by understanding who this simple, ordinary man was and how his example can help us hear God's call.

Next to Mary, St. Joseph is the person who spent the most time with Jesus in his early formative years. We don't know the names of Joseph's parents – we know only that he was of the house of David through the line of King Solomon. We don't know when he was born or when he died. The Gospel of Mark doesn't talk about him. Within the Gospel of John, he is mentioned only twice (John 1:45, 6:42). The Gospels of Matthew and Luke are our principal sources for the childhood of Jesus and what little we know of Joseph. While Joseph's story is mainly untold in scripture, his very name is rich in meaning. The name Joseph means "God will increase" or "to add or increase."

It is especially striking to note, as we try to understand who Joseph was, that there are no direct words spoken by Joseph in scripture. There are no Psalms, no lamentations, and no lengthy dialogues revealing his inner heart. So how, then, does he speak to us today? Through his actions! Everything we know about Joseph comes from his actions, which reveal an openness and willingness towards God's call.

We learn about Joseph through his dreams and encounters with angels. As we have seen, dreams are one of God's chosen methods of communication. Three times in the Gospels, the angel of God visits Joseph in a dream. In the first dream, the angel comes to tell Joseph to take Mary, who is pregnant, as his wife. In the second dream, he is told to flee with Mary and Jesus to Egypt to escape Herod's decree to kill all male Hebrew babies. In the third and final dream, the angel instructs Joseph to return to Galilee and build his family home in Nazareth.

In each of these dreams, Joseph opened his heart to the words of God, freely accepting the messages and acting upon them without question. He could not have done this without a strong faith in God. In many ways, Joseph's complete trust in God and the obedient response of his actions parallels Mary's "yes" to God in the Annunciation. Both opened their hearts fully to God's wishes.

Scripture also tells us that Joseph was a carpenter by trade, that he was a just and pious man and a devoted husband and foster father. He was open to God's word and was willing to carry it out regardless of the personal cost.

The Holy Family's years in Nazareth are not documented in any of the Gospels, but we can surmise that, as a child, Jesus would have spent long hours working alongside Joseph in the carpentry shop, where Joseph's influence would have helped form and shape Jesus as he grew. The last mention of Joseph is when Jesus goes missing at the age of twelve, after Mary and Joseph have gone with him to Jerusalem. We hear of Joseph's concern for Jesus as the desperate parents search for their son, and witness Joseph's puzzlement when Jesus is found in the temple, talking with the learned scribes and teachers there. After this moment, Joseph is not mentioned again.

One of the challenges of modern fatherhood is simply being present to those who love us. It is not news that the heavy demands of the workplace and professional networks pressure many men to scrimp on the time they give to their families. And even fatherhood itself has become a diminished currency in certain segments of society and is sometimes viewed as an unnecessary appendage to family life. To this Joseph presents a challenge: he is always there when needed, fulfilling his responsibilities to those who need him. He does it without question. In fact, for him there is no question – his family comes first. There is no agonizing over what this may do to his career or whether it is personally fulfilling. He just does what needs to be done.

Moreover, St. Joseph shows us that words are not the only way to express our faith: through our actions, God sees clearly what is in our hearts. The heart is a vulnerable part of us; we are often afraid to express our inner feelings. But Joseph did just that! He had the courage to be submissive to God and to God's will, even when he had other choices – after all, the law and his peers would have supported him had he rejected Mary and turned her away after finding out that she was with child. Instead, he took the more difficult path that God opened for him.

In doing so, he turned his life and decision making over to God, just as Mary did when she said, "Let it be done unto me according to your word" at the Annunciation. Joseph opened the door of his heart to the will of God, allowing God to enter into his heart and direct his life.

In art, we often see the image of Christ knocking at the door. Is this door the door of our heart? He knocks until we answer. "Listen! I am standing at the door, knocking; if you hear my voice and open the door, I will come in to you and eat with you, and you with me" (Revelation 3:20). Because Joseph was willing to unlock the door to his heart and let the Lord enter, he received the grace of God. Are we prepared to do the same?

## Reflection Questions

*St. Joseph was an ordinary sort of man on whom God relied to do great things. He did exactly what the Lord wanted him to do, in each and every event that went to make up his life.*

Blessed Josemaria Escriva

1. How do you barricade the doors of your heart against God? How can you begin to open those doors?

2. Is your heart as open as Joseph's to the call of God? If not, how can following Joseph's example help you?

3. Are you willing to respond through your actions to the message of the Gospel? Name three concrete actions you can take to spread God's message of love for all people.

# LET US PRAY +

Gracious God,
so often our hearts are hardened
by the actions of the world,
where injustice and selfishness too often rule.
Strengthen our faith, we pray,
that it will be the key that opens the door to our hearts.
In opening our hearts and minds to your will,
may we, like Joseph, place all our trust in you.
We ask this through Christ our Lord.
Amen. +

# Nicodemus

### *Being a man who is not afraid to question*

*The light shines in the darkness,*
*and the darkness has not overcome it.*

John 1:5

I n many cases, the lives of these men after God's own heart can be summed up in a few words. Jacob struggled; Daniel dared; Joseph trusted. The life of Nicodemus can be summed up as "emerging from darkness" – both literal and symbolic darkness.

The Gospel of John presents Nicodemus as a model of faith and courage for all of us today. Here we will focus on the images of darkness and light that John's Gospel offers.

Nicodemus was a Pharisee, a member of the prestigious governing council known as the Sanhedrin – the very council that would eventually charge and execute Jesus. The Sanhedrin was the highest legal and judicial body of the Jewish community. As a member of this council, Nicodemus held an important position within the community. He was a respected teacher who enjoyed a very nice lifestyle. Although he was a Pharisee, he was not blinded by his own religious tradition. He was an intelligent man who could not overlook the signs that seemed to indicate the divinity of Christ. He could see from the signs and actions of Jesus that truly he must be from God. Yet even knowing all of this and seeing the signs, Nicodemus needed a direct encounter with Christ to bring clarity and light to what he knew.

Nicodemus appears three times in the Gospel of John (chapter 3; 7:50-52; 19:39). The first time, he comes to visit Jesus by night; the second time, he comes to Jesus' defense against the accusations of the Pharisees; and the third time, he is helping Joseph of Arimathea to bury Jesus.

In his first encounter with Jesus, as Nicodemus arrives under the cover of darkness, the image of darkness has several different meanings. In the literal sense, Nicodemus chose to visit Jesus at night so his colleagues wouldn't find out. The members of the Sanhedrin, who clearly found Jesus to be a problem, would not have approved of such a meeting. Yet Nicodemus was open to the teachings of Jesus and wanted to encounter this man for himself. He acknowledged him as a great teacher (Rabbi) but wasn't ready to admit his beliefs openly.

Nicodemus also comes to Jesus in a state of spiritual darkness, seeking illumination (light) through the words of Jesus. As Jesus speaks of life, faith and eternal life, Nicodemus gradually emerges from his personal darkness and begins to see the light.

Although he did not fully understand the teachings of Jesus, he was willing and open to growing in understanding. When

Jesus tells Nicodemus that in order to truly know the Lord he had to be born again, Nicodemus takes Jesus' words literally and fails to understand them fully. To Nicodemus it seems impossible for a grown man to re-enter his mother's womb in order to be born again. Jesus explains to him,

> "Very truly, I tell you, no one can enter the kingdom of God without being born of water and Spirit. What is born of the flesh is flesh, and what is born of the Spirit is spirit. Do not be astonished that I said to you, 'You must be born from above.' The wind blows where it chooses, and you hear the sound of it, but you do not know where it comes from or where it goes. So it is with everyone who is born of the Spirit." (John 3:5-8)

He was telling Nicodemus that our salvation comes from our direct encounter with Jesus. Nicodemus learns that he must forsake everything he stands for – undergo a spiritual rebirth and turn away from the only life he knows.

After this initial encounter with Jesus, Nicodemus never again hid in the darkness; the other two appearances of Nicodemus in the Gospel – in support of Jesus during the trial before the Sanhedrin, and in respectfully assisting Joseph of Arimathea to bury Jesus – are both highly public events.

The story of Nicodemus and his journey towards spiritual enlightenment has much to say to us today. We, like Nicodemus, often exist in a world of darkness, allowing the world around us to influence and overtake our personal encounter or relationship with God. Like Nicodemus, we must be prepared to undergo a spiritual rebirth, acknowledging our failures and our weaknesses and experiencing a conversion of mind and heart.

Nicodemus was a believer, but at first he was not willing to let his beliefs affect his job. He wasn't willing to put his career on the line or to face the ridicule of his colleagues. It wasn't that he didn't believe in Jesus; he did! It wasn't that he didn't care for Jesus; he did! What he lacked prior to his direct encounter with Christ was the courage to commit fully to Christ.

Sound familiar? How often do we walk in the darkness of spiritual loneliness, afraid to acknowledge the important role that Christ plays in our lives for fear of what others might say or think about us?

Yet as Christians, we know where to find the light. We know the source of enlightenment and insight: Christ is the light of the world. Through our direct, personal encounter with Christ, we find the light that will strengthen and guide us in all we do and say.

In today's world, amid the darkness of violence, intolerance and greed, Christ's light is always shining through. We are called not only to see that light but to reflect it for others, for as Christ reminds us, "You are the light of the world" (Matthew 5:14).

This means letting the light of Christ shine ever brighter in our lives – not only in our homes and churches, but everywhere we are. We, like Nicodemus, may come to our relationship with Christ in the darkness, but through our willingness to encounter Christ we move forward into the light. By opening his heart and mind to the Lord, Nicodemus represents a challenge to us to be a little slower to judge and wrap ourselves in our own prejudices.

Jesus calls us to public ministry; to be light to the world; to be filled with the light of God and in turn to help dispel the darkness of the age. "In the same way, let your light shine before others, so that they may see your good works and give glory to your Father in heaven" (Matthew 14:16).

How do we do this?

We walk in the way and in the word of God. We follow God's example and become light to others as we help to bring about the kingdom of God by welcoming strangers, befriending those who are lonely, working with and for the poor and disenfranchised, and offering our gifts to those in need. Through our words and actions, we can lift the spirits and brighten the world of those who are suffering in any way. As the Rite of Christian Burial reminds us, "My friends, let every mark of affection and every gesture of friendship that you give to others be a sign of God's peace for you."

## Reflection Questions

*"What I say to you in the dark, tell in the light;
and what you hear whispered, proclaim from the housetops."*
Matthew 10:27

1. Do you hide your faith in the darkness of the night? How can you move from darkness to light in your relationship with God?

2. Nicodemus had faith but was afraid to acknowledge it. Do you hide your relationship with God from others, or do you allow the light of Christ to be reflected in all you do?

3. What can you do to dispel the darkness you find in the world around you? Name three concrete actions you can take and think about how you can carry them out.

## LET US PRAY +

Heavenly Father,
so often we, like Nicodemus, come to you in darkness.
Grant that through our perseverance
and our desire to know you more fully,
that darkness will be replaced with the light of your love.
Grant also that we may reflect this light in our daily lives,
living as a true reflection of your love to all we meet.
We ask this through Christ our Lord,
the light of the world.
Amen. +

# Zaccheus

## *Being a man who is an outcast*

*When Jesus came to the place, he looked up and said to him,*
*"Zaccheus, hurry and come down; for I must stay at*
*your house today."*

Luke 19:5

With the above words, Jesus calls Zaccheus. Had Zaccheus's heart not been open and seeking God, he would not have heard the call, but God had a plan for this strange little outcast man. His encounter with Jesus was the first step in his conversion journey.

Zaccheus may seem like an odd addition to our selection of role models for how to live as a man after God's own heart, but Zaccheus reminds us that even the most challenged heart is vulnerable to conversion and God's call.

Before we look at Zaccheus's conversion, we need to get to know him. His journey was not an easy one, for he was out of sync with his faith. He was a Jew by birth, but when we meet him in the scriptures, he is the chief tax collector (Luke 19:2).

At this point in history, comparisons were often made between the Pharisees, who were righteous men, and the tax collectors, who were sinners. These Jews collected taxes from their own people on behalf of the Romans. Those chosen for this job tended to be outcasts: other Jews despised them for working for the enemy, which included swearing an oath of respect and honour to the Roman emperor and participating in pagan rituals. Many of them, including Zacchaeus, the "chief," became rich at the expense of their brothers and sisters by charging even more than required and pocketing the difference. They made life for their own countrymen painfully oppressive. And because they were Jewish, tax collectors were never fully accepted by the Romans.

All of this and more applies to Zacchaeus. He had participated fully in this Roman initiative, from pagan sacrifices and oaths to forcing his own people to pay exorbitant taxes, which eventually made him a rich man. Not only was he an outcast, he was a traitor to his people. Still, he achieved what he thought he wanted most: great wealth. Like many people today, Zacchaeus thought that happiness and peace of mind came with money and possessions.

Yet when Zacchaeus heard that Jesus would be coming through his town, he felt drawn to go and see Jesus for himself. Because he was short and there was a large crowd, he knew he would never get to see Jesus as he passed by. Yet this desire to see Jesus was powerful indeed: he was so determined to see Jesus, he ran on ahead and climbed a sycamore tree. He could see everything from his perch and be somewhat hidden at the same time.

Imagine Zacchaeus's surprise when Jesus stopped, looked up into the tree and called Zacchaeus down, saying, "I must stay at your house today" (Luke 19:5). It is this call to stay awhile with Christ that we are all searching for. When Christ enters into our home and our hearts to abide there, our conversion begins. God never forces himself into the heart but waits for the willing, receptive heart to be open to receiving him. There are no restrictions on who can and who cannot receive the Lord in their heart. Saint and sinner alike are called equally, and each opens their heart in their own time. The more time we spend staying with Christ, the greater our transformation.

The story of Zacchaeus reminds me of the story of the lost sheep (Luke 15:3-7). In this parable, Jesus asks, "Which one of you, having a hundred sheep and losing one of them, does not leave the ninety-nine in the wilderness and go after the one that is lost until he finds it?" In just such a way, Jesus searches out Zacchaeus. While there were many followers and supporters gathered to meet and see Jesus as he travelled through the town, it was not to these faithful followers and their homes that he was drawn. He was drawn to the lost sheep, Zacchaeus, who needed to be brought home. The shepherd knows his sheep. He knew Zacchaeus's name and knew that he needed to spend time with him to help bring him back into the fold. And so it began. Jesus went with Zacchaeus to his home and there he preached the Gospel to Zacchaeus.

Our own stories are not so different. Our economy offers unimaginable wealth to those willing to sacrifice everything human about themselves to a single-minded ambition for riches. And wealth can come in forms other than money: influence and power over others, celebrity and popularity are just as heady temptations as financial success. To be a Zacchaeus today is not a stretch.

We, too, must answer the call and invite the Lord into our hearts before transformation can occur. There is an urgency in the call of the Lord to Zacchaeus when he says, "I must stay at your house today" – not later, not in a while, but today. God wants us to be open to him whatever our stage and state of life. He is not waiting for perfection – he wants us in all our brokenness and sinful state. He wants us today!

Zacchaeus's transformation was swifter than most. Following Christ breaking open the scriptures and preaching the Gospel to him, Zacchaeus gave half his possessions to the poor and promised to pay back everyone he had cheated four times what he owed! Having worshipped money and material goods, he discovered through his personal encounter with Christ that these things were, in fact, idols that kept him from his relationship with God. In freeing himself of these earthly chains, he opened himself up to receiving Christ in his heart.

This willingness to give up earthly possessions and desires for the hidden treasure of a life in Christ requires great faith and trust that God will provide. You will notice that Christ didn't ask Zacchaeus to give everything up – it was his own choice to make restitution. This change of heart, this conversion, came about automatically as a result of Zacchaeus's encounter with Christ.

We are all called to encounter Christ. We are made rich in our love of Christ, for "one's life does not consist in the abundance of possessions" (Luke 12:15).

We learn so much from Zacchaeus. He shows us that we need to constantly re-evaluate our priorities. This is a story of change: it makes clear that our present and future lives do not need to be controlled by past actions. We need to understand the difference between wants and needs. Our desire for more and more things moves us further away from an authentic relationship with Christ. The desire for material goods and things of this world blind us to the joy of salvation in Christ. Thomas Merton, a Trappist monk and a great Catholic thinker and writer, could easily have been speaking about Zacchaeus when he said in his book *He Is Risen*, "True encounter with Christ liberated something in us, a power we did not know we had, a hope; a capacity for life, a resilience; an ability to bounce back when we thought we were completely defeated, a capacity to grow and change, a power of creative transformation." Indeed, he could easily have been speaking about us!

## Reflection Questions

*"Zacchaeus, hurry and come down ...."* (Luke 19:5)

1. Many people question where God is in their lives, but unlike Zacchaeus, they don't go looking for him. How can you seek God in your daily life?

2. What things are holding you back from being open to a deeper relationship with God? What are these earthly chains that bind you? What can you do to help break these chains and free yourself to develop your relationship with God?

3. Where can you go for help to tackle those chains? What resources does our Church provide to face this challenge?

## LET US PRAY +

Heavenly Father,
we are chained to our earthly existence
with chains that we forge ourselves.
Help us, we pray, to break free from these chains
so that we might soar in our relationship with you.
Strengthen us as we struggle to free ourselves
in order that we might encounter you more fully
in our daily lives.
Be with us, guide us and fill us with your love.
We ask these things through Christ our Lord.
Amen. +

# The Centurion

## *Being a man of deep faith*

*The centurion sent friends to say to him, "Lord, do not trouble yourself, for I am not worthy to have you come under my roof; therefore I did not presume to come to you. But only speak the word, and let my servant be healed. For I also am a man set under authority, with soldiers under me; and I say to one, 'Go', and he goes, and to another, 'Come', and he comes, and to my slave, 'Do this', and the slave does it."*

Luke 7:6-8

A s we read the New Testament we see, hear and learn indirectly about the Roman army, the soldiers and the centurions. In total, we meet seven centurions in these scriptures, all men of commendable standing within the Roman army. In this chapter we will look at two who speak to us today.

To be a centurion was both a great honour and a privilege that was earned with hard work, dedication and courage. Centurions, who were considered the backbone of the Roman army, would have received twenty times the amount paid to an

ordinary soldier. Today we might call them middle manage-
ment, as they were in charge of hundreds of working soldiers
and answered to a higher military authority. You may well ask,
what could a pagan soldier tell us about being a man after God's
own heart?

The two we will explore from scripture have admirable qualities that merit our consideration as Catholic men today. The first
one visits Jesus because of a sick servant; the second supervised
the crucifixion of Christ.

## The centurion whose servant is sick

The first centurion that we meet utters the words found at
the start of this chapter: "I am not worthy to have you come
under my roof..." – words that we echo today in the Eucharist.
We, like the centurion, acknowledge that we come to God in our
unworthiness, but we believe, as the centurion did, that Christ
has only to say the word and we will be healed.

There are two parallel accounts of this encounter with the
centurion in scripture: Matthew 8:5-13 and Luke 7:1-10. In
Luke's Gospel, we learn that the centurion was a pagan and a
member of the Roman military, but had a positive relationship
with the Jewish community. He was, in fact, responsible for the
building of their synagogue. In this telling of the story, the centurion sends others to Jesus to speak for him; out of humility,
he did not feel worthy to address Jesus face to face to heal the
servant. He had faith in the power and authority of Christ, but
felt unworthy to approach him. In the Gospel of Matthew, the

centurion appeals to Jesus directly and knows Jesus can heal the servant, but still feels unworthy for Christ to come to his home. What is obvious in both accounts is that the centurion, unlike many Jewish people, recognized the authority and power of Christ. As Matthew's Gospel tells us, Jesus recognizes the centurion's great faith by saying, "I tell you, not even in Israel have I found such faith."

From this story we learn that faith shows respect and honour for God's authority and as such is pleasing to God. God takes great delight in our faithful response to his call. Strong faith, like that of the centurion, requires no tangible proof, for faith is a deep, abiding trust that transcends the visible. It was in hearing the word of God that the centurion found the faith and courage to ask for healing for his servant. We must follow this example of hearing God's word and allowing it to rest in our heart so that our faith will be strong and we will be willing to ask for God's healing touch.

Finally, it is in his "I am not worthy" comment that the centurion speaks most directly to us today. Despite his position of power, control and authority over Jesus, this Roman centurion came before him acknowledging his own humility. He acknowledged that he was not worthy of receiving help from Christ, yet believed that Christ could and would help his servant. How did the centurion know this? He didn't! He had faith that Christ's help transcended all political, cultural and physical limitations and that with but a word, Christ could make his servant whole.

At Mass, every time we utter the words "Lord, I am not worthy that you should enter under my roof, but only say the word and my soul shall be healed," we say we have this same faith. What a beautiful acknowledgment of our faith and trust in God!

As we move further through this Gospel story, we see that Christ was amazed by the centurion's faith. As a result of this tremendous act of faith, the centurion's servant was healed.

## The centurion at the cross

Perhaps one of the briefest encounters with Jesus is that of the centurion who is at the foot of the cross at the crucifixion. We don't know if he is the same one who also humbly asked Christ to heal his servant, or the centurion Cornelius from the Acts of the Apostles, or another person entirely. All we know is that he was there to supervise the crucifixion. He would have watched and participated in many crucifixions throughout his career, and yet this was different. The earth shook, the sun turned black and he looked into the face of Christ. The centurion was obviously terrified and yet overpowered by what he was experiencing. The words he spoke when Jesus died resound through the ages: "Truly this man was God's son!" Here is the first revelation of Christ's divinity by a human being. It is profoundly moving that the first person to acknowledge the divinity of Christ was a gentile and a Roman soldier.

This centurion appears in the Gospels of Matthew, Mark and Luke. In each Gospel his words are slightly different, but all essentially reinforce the concept of Christ's true identity. Looking into the face of Christ is what brings clarity for the centurion at the cross. In this encounter with Christ, he sees and believes in the Son of God.

The centurions have many parallels today. Indeed, we hold soldiers in high esteem and the higher the rank, the higher the esteem. We value decisiveness, loyalty and integrity – the same attributes we admire in military officers – and see them in our favourite heroes of the sports and corporate worlds. Men today instinctively "get" what the centurions were about. We can appreciate what they saw in Christ. We are called to this same encounter: to see the face of Christ and to acknowledge him as our saviour.

## Reflection Questions

*"Truly this man was God's Son!"* (Mark 15:39)

1. Do you look for tangible evidence of God's existence or can you rest in the knowledge and faith that God is present in your life?

2. Within your daily work, whether in the workforce or as a volunteer, how can you actively seek the face of God in those you encounter?

3. Like the two centurions we explored in this chapter, we are changed by our encounter with the Lord. How have you helped foster a sense of ongoing encounter with Christ with your family, friends and colleagues?

# LET US PRAY +

Gracious God,

through our personal encounters with you,

we are called to live in faith as your sons.

May we, like the centurion whose servant needed healing,

trust in the power of your word,

and like the centurion at the foot of the cross,

recognize the true identity of Christ.

We ask this through Christ our Lord.

Amen. +

# St. Peter

*Being a man of contradiction*

*The Lord said to him, "And I tell you, you are Peter,
and on this rock I will build my church,
and the gates of Hades will not prevail against it."*

Matthew 16:18-19

P eter is a key role model for Catholic men today. Like many of the men described in this book, he was prone to making mistakes and was often chastised by Christ. And yet, he was and is a great example for us to follow.

Peter was an ordinary man, as scripture tells us: "Now when they saw the boldness of Peter and John and realized that they were uneducated and ordinary men…" (Acts 4:13). Peter was a man's man. He loved the chaos, the commotion, the hustle and bustle of daily life. He loved to be in the thick of things. Some people have said he was a man of action and not a thinker. Many of us would describe ourselves the same way.

Peter is one of the most fully fleshed-out characters in the Bible. We usually hear the story of a particular person and then never hear of them again. In Peter's case, we get to know a great deal about who he is and what makes him tick. Through the four Gospels, the Acts of the Apostles and the two letters that bear his name, we see many sides of this man of contradictions.

He was a simple man, a fisherman, who met Jesus and willingly followed him to become a "fisher of men." Very early on, Peter was recognized as a leader, the first among the apostles. He quickly became their spokesman and Jesus' right-hand man.

What do we learn about Peter that speaks to us today as we grow in our relationship with Christ? Like each of us, Peter wants to follow in Jesus' footsteps. He wants to do the right thing. He has faith, but at times he runs away from the challenges he faces because he feels he has to face them alone. He (like us) fails to recognize that God is always with us, ready to support us in all our daily living. Over time, Peter grew in faith and understanding, due to the fact that his eyes and ears were always open to learning and his heart was ready and willing to receive Christ's teachings.

We see in the Gospel of Matthew that, while Peter was a man of great courage, he was also easily terrified.

Peter answered [Jesus], "Lord, if it is you, command me to come to you on the water." [Jesus] said, "Come." So Peter got out of the boat, started walking on the water, and came toward Jesus. But when he noticed the strong wind, he became frightened, and beginning to sink, he cried out, "Lord, save me!" Jesus immediately reached out his hand and caught him, saying to him, "You of little faith, why did you doubt?" (Matthew 14:28-31)

Peter shows us, in the story of leaping out of the boat to walk on the water, that pride in our own actions must never supersede our trust and faith in Jesus. We must never rely solely on our own strength or courage, for without Jesus we can become weak and vulnerable at any time. Peter, the man of action, left the boat filled with courage, and yet quickly became afraid because he had lost his trust in Jesus and began to sink. In that moment he realized the power of Christ to save and protect him, and so called out to Christ. Jesus reached out and saved him, re-establishing the faith connection.

Peter wanted to be strong, courageous and committed, and he was all of these things, but at times he was weak, cowardly and indecisive. Sound familiar? In our bravado and certitude we sometimes forget that it is through our faith in Christ that all things are possible, that we can face the trials and tribulations of our lives because our faith will get us through those difficult times. While we may not literally be walking on water, it is clear that without our faith we will sink into our greatest fears and troubles. When we live in faith, the troubles may still be there but we will have the strength we need to face them.

In Peter we see the coming together of various gifts of the Holy Spirit – knowledge, wisdom, understanding, courage, right judgment, reverence, and wonder and awe. These gifts, which we also need to rely on in our faith journey, do not exist in isolation but are interwoven, becoming the fabric of our daily lives and a solid foundation on which our faith grows and develops.

In a moment of great strength and faith, Peter says to Jesus, "Even though I must die with you, I will not deny you" (Matthew 26:35). A powerful statement that we would all want to make! Yet Peter's weakness or lack of courage surfaces after Jesus is arrested. When asked if he knows Jesus, Peter denies it three times out of fear for his own safety. As soon as he realizes what he has done, he weeps bitterly. It is in this moment that Peter's great love for Christ is revealed.

Despite his denial of Christ, it was to Peter that Jesus first revealed himself following the resurrection (1 Corinthians 15:5). Peter's weaknesses were overcome by his faith in Jesus – a good lesson for all of us that we can move forward after making mistakes!

Peter's powerful experience of reconciliation and repentance takes place on the shores of the Sea of Tiberius when the resurrected Christ prepares breakfast for his disciples.

When they had finished breakfast, Jesus said to Simon Peter, "Simon son of John, do you love me more than these?" He said to him, "Yes, Lord; you know that I love you." Jesus said to him, "Feed my lambs." A second time he said to him, "Simon son of John, do you love me?" He said to him, "Yes, Lord; you know that I love you." Jesus said to him, "Tend my sheep." He said to him the third time, "Simon son of John, do you love me?" Peter felt hurt because he said to him the third time, "Do you love me?" And he said to him, "Lord, you know everything; you know that I love you." Jesus said to him, "Feed my sheep." (John 21:15-17)

Three times Peter was given the opportunity to express his love for Christ. Many have said this was the act of reconciliation for the three times Peter denied Christ.

Jesus has forgiven him for his actions. In this way, Peter offers us a strong example of the power of reconciliation: that Jesus, regardless of our failings, welcomes us back lovingly into the fold. Peter's greatest weakness – denying that he knew Jesus – becomes for us an inspiring reminder of the beauty of God's mercy and of the sacrament of reconciliation.

Could there be any greater sin than denying our saviour? Yet Jesus forgave Peter and used his strengths to build his earthly church, making Peter the first pope. If Christ can reconcile Peter's failings and God can use him to help bring the Good News of God's love to the world, we are reassured that, through reconciliation and God's forgiveness, we can grow in our relationship with God.

We must never count on ourselves more than we count on the grace of God as revealed in Christ. We see this in Peter's actions on the stormy sea and in his denial of Christ. Peter shows us that while we may be men of action and courage, we are human, and at times we will falter and fail. Even so, Christ will always be willing to welcome us back through the sacrament of reconciliation. In seeking to be reconciled with God, our faith grows stronger and our relationship with God deepens.

# Reflection Questions

*Like Peter, as flawed individuals, we need to constantly remind ourselves that God wants us in our brokenness. God calls us into this relationship whenever we are ready. God is always ready to receive us. He has made the first move – all we have to do is respond.*

1. How have you responded to God's call?

2. Have you, like Peter, lost faith in God's ability to save and protect you? How can you overcome this lack of faith?

3. How can celebrating the sacrament of reconciliation help you move closer to God?

# LET US PRAY +

Gracious and loving God,

you had the patience to forgive and shape St. Peter

into the apostle of the apostles.

Grant that we may follow in his footsteps

as we build a solid foundation on which to grow in faith.

Help us to fully appreciate

the joy and beauty of reconciliation with you

as you offer us your unending mercy.

Be with us each day as we journey

as pilgrims on the way of Christ.

We ask this through Christ our Lord.

Amen. +

# Men of the Modern Age

# St. Thomas More

## Being a man of principle

*"I die the King's good servant, and God's first."*

Thomas More, on the scaffold
July 16, 1535

S t. Thomas More is the subject of many books as well as movies and plays. Born on February 7, 1477, he was the son of a lawyer – a commoner with no noble pedigree. Throughout his life he readily identified with the poor and those who suffered at the hands of the powerful.

He struggled with whether to enter religious life, but in the end chose the path of the laity. A naturally kind man, his hallmarks were truth and justice. He completed his law education at Oxford University at the age of 32, married and had four children. As an administrator, judge, counsellor and scholar, he gained the attention and friendship of King Henry VIII during what were turbulent social and political times. The king, unhappy that his wife could not bear him a male heir, wanted a divorce so he could marry another. Obviously, the Catholic Church opposed this idea.

But Henry was determined to get a divorce by whatever means necessary. He appointed Thomas More as Lord Chamberlain (replacing Cardinal Wolsey) in the hopes that he was placing a friend in what was considered the highest-ranking role in the government of the time. Henry knew that Thomas, a devout Catholic, would not support the divorce and remarriage, but hoped that he could be convinced not to object – that Henry would be able to get around Thomas's objections. After much political intrigue and upheaval, Henry split from the Catholic Church to establish the Church of England, of which he would be the Head. All members of the government were asked to sign and swear an oath that Henry VIII was to be the supreme head of the Catholic Church in England. Thomas refused! He did not judge, cajole or berate Henry; he simply refused to sign. Thomas remained true and obedient to his God. He tried to understand what was being asked of him, but felt that his obedience belonged first and foremost to God and Church teaching, not to anyone of this world. He always maintained that he was the King's good servant but that he was God's servant first. It was Thomas More's belief that he served God the King under whom all other kings must bow in obedience. When Henry asked for his life if he wouldn't sign the oath, Thomas chose to suffer the death of a martyr rather than renounce his religious principles.

We see in Thomas More an exceptionally devout Catholic given to much prayer and study of scripture. His detailed knowledge of sacred scripture was another of his powerful weapons in his struggle with King Henry and the heresies of the times. In fact, Thomas More widely promoted the study of scripture. "Holy

Scripture is the highest and best learning that any man can have, if one takes the right way in the learning. It is so marvellously well-tempered that a mouse may wade therein and an elephant be drowned therein." (T.E. Bridgett, *Life and Writings of Sir Thomas More* [London 1892], 307.)

We hear a lot of scripture at Mass. A major part of the Mass – the Liturgy of the Word – comes directly from scripture. During the Liturgy of the Word, we hear a reading from the Old Testament (or from the Acts of the Apostles, in the Easter Season), a Psalm, part of a New Testament letter, and a reading from one of the four Gospels. The Sunday readings are organized into a three-year cycle; over the three years, we hear selections from all four Gospels and many other biblical books. Not only the readings but many of the responses and words of the Eucharistic celebration are taken directly from scripture.

But we need to study scripture as well as hear it proclaimed at Mass. Thomas More emphasized the need to read scripture in the light of faith, which is a very powerful message and model for us today. We need to find time to sit with our sacred scriptures and allow the word of God to speak to us.

Thomas More used scripture to inform, enlighten and transform his thinking and to strengthen his faith in and obedience to God. We must do the same. St. Jerome, one of the great thinkers of our Church, said in his commentary on the Book of Isaiah, "Ignorance of Scripture is indeed ignorance of Christ." The life of Thomas More reminds us to look to the talents and gifts that God has given us in order to know how we are to act with faith and obedience. More reminds us to use the gifts of the Holy Spirit that we received in our baptism and that were strengthened through the sacrament of confirmation: knowledge, understanding and wisdom; courage and right judgment; wonder and awe and fear of the Lord. Each of these God-given gifts is meant to be unpacked and used as we live our faith in the service of all, as Thomas More did.

His knowledge, wisdom and understanding of the difficult times in his turbulent history led him to have the courage and right judgment to make informed decisions. Even though he was a powerful secular leader, with all the temptations that entailed, his sense of wonder and awe and sincere fear of the Lord served to reinforce his obedience to the will of God. He was called to defend his faith and defend it he did, even unto death. Like Thomas, we are called to be obedient, to listen to the word of God through the scriptures and to share the graces received freely with others.

## Reflection Questions

"*I believe, when statesmen forsake their own private conscience for the sake of their public duties, they lead their country by a short route to chaos.*"
Sir Thomas More, *A Man for All Seasons*, Act One

1. When faced with difficult moral or ethical questions that challenge your beliefs and the teachings of the Church, what sustains and supports you?  →

2. Reflect on the gifts of the Holy Spirit (knowledge, understanding, wisdom, courage, right judgment, wonder and awe, and fear of the Lord) that were strengthened for you at your confirmation. Which of these gifts are you using in your daily life?

3. Which of these gifts of the Holy Spirit do you need to unpack in your life?

## LET US PRAY +

Heavenly Father,
grant that we, like your humble servant St. Thomas More,
might have the knowledge of our tradition,
the understanding of our teachings
and the wisdom to apply them in our daily lives.
May we have the courage and right judgment
to stand up for our faith,
to acknowledge the wonder and awe
of your presence in our lives
and to be ever obedient to your Word.
We ask this through Christ our Lord.
Amen. +

# Blessed Pier Giorgio Frassati

*Being a man of virtue and a model of the Beatitudes*

*To live without faith, without a patrimony to defend,*
*without a steady struggle for truth,*
*that is not living, but existing.*

Pier Giorgio Frassati

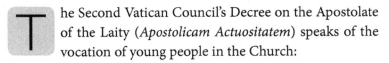

he Second Vatican Council's Decree on the Apostolate of the Laity (*Apostolicam Actuositatem*) speaks of the vocation of young people in the Church:

[They] exert a very important influence on modern society … Their heightened influence … demands of them a proportionate apostolic activity, but their natural qualities also fit them for this activity. As they become more conscious of their own personalities, they are impelled by a zest for life and a ready eagerness to assume their own responsibility, and they yearn to play their part in social and cultural life. If this spirit is imbued with the Spirit of Christ and is inspired by obedience and love of the Church, it can be expected to be very fruitful. They should be the first to carry the apostolate directly to other young persons, connecting their apostolic efforts within their circle, according to the needs of the social environment in which they live. (no. 12)

Six decades before Vatican II, Pier Giorgio Frassati lived out the Christian vocation as laid out in this decree. He listened to the invitation of Christ to "Follow me" (Matthew 4:18-20).

Frassati was born in Turin, Italy, on April 6, 1901. His mother, Adelaide, was a devout Catholic and painter, while his father, Alfredo, was an agnostic and a very influential journalist who founded the newspaper *La Stampa*. Both parents were confounded by the deep spirituality that Pier Giorgio developed at an early age.

His early years at school were not easy, as Pier Giorgio was much more interested in sports than in academics – until he entered a private Jesuit-run school. With their support and encouragement, he managed to complete his academic work. It was during these years that he developed a rich spiritual life. At a time when it was not at all normative or widely accepted, he received communion every day. As well as this deep devotion to the Eucharist, Pier Giorgio had a profound devotion for the Blessed Virgin Mary.

At the age of seventeen, he joined the St. Vincent de Paul Society and worked tirelessly as a volunteer with the sick, the needy and especially with servicemen and their families as they returned from World War I.

He entered the Royal Polytechnical University of Turin, where he studied to become a mining engineer. As he told his friends, he was to serve Christ among the miners. During his student days at the university, Pier Giorgio developed a strong sense of social and political activism. For him, charity was not enough; what was needed was social reform. While still a student, he promoted Catholic Social Teaching based on the writings and principles of Pope Leo XIII, as expressed in the pope's 1891 encyclical *Rerum Novarum* (On Capital and Labour).

Pier Giorgio had a very strong sense of responsibility towards the poor. Countless stories describe his anonymous philanthropic gestures to Turin's poorest inhabitants. Not only was he prepared to give all that he could materially, such as food, clothing and medicine, but he gave of himself. He understood the personal meaning of the Eucharist, but knew it was much more than a private devotion – for those who receive the Eucharist have a responsibility to share the graces received with the entire world.

Pier Giorgio's life was cut short when he died from complications from polio on July 4, 1928. He was 24 years old. He may have contracted the disease from the sick for whom he cared. Yet even in his final, painful days, his thoughts and instructions were for the sick and what needed to be done for them upon his death.

What in the life of Pier Giorgio Frassati speaks to us today? What did God see in the heart of this young man? The most striking image that comes to mind is in the portrait of Pier Giorgio that was unveiled when Pope John Paul II declared him Blessed on May 20, 1990. This was not a typical saintly portrait of a man at prayer or even resting in contemplative thought. No, this was the image of a strong, vital young man dressed in mountain climbing gear with one foot firmly planted on a rock – the image of a successful climber.

This image of the mountain and the climber speaks volumes about Pier Giorgio, both literally and figuratively. From a very early age, he was an avid climber. As a member of the Italian Alpine Club, he climbed many major mountain ranges, facing countless challenges along the way. These mountains allowed him to test his athletic ability and to build friendships with those who joined him in these activities. He never failed to use these opportunities to encourage, support and nurture those less skilled than himself as well as to share his faith through both prayer and action. For Pier Giorgio, it was never enough to simply know the faith; faith must be lived out in one's actions.

Pier Giorgio's mountains also represented a place for learning, worship, and physical and mental exercise. He was always helping his peers to strive for the top in their physical and spiritual lives. *Verso l'alto,* which means "toward the top," became the motto for his life.

Through his example, we see the need to constantly look for ways to enhance our relationships with our families and friends as well as with those whom we are called to serve – the poor and the outcast. Most importantly, his example pushes us to consider how we can move forward in our relationship with God. The challenge is to be the best we can be on both a personal and a communal level. We are encouraged to strive for perfection in all we do.

You'll notice it is "strive for" perfection, not achieve perfection, which for humans would be impossible. We are simply called to constantly move forward in our attempt to become more Christ-like in all we do. And so it is that Pier Giorgio Frassati models for all of us, especially young adult men, to be more connected to our faith, to our God, to the poor, and to our family and friends.

Pier Giorgio seemed able to find balance in the social, spiritual and service-oriented aspects of his life. Finding balance is a challenge most of us face today. We struggle with the many roles that we are called to fill each day as sons, fathers, husbands, co-workers and friends. Still, we must push ourselves to find time to sit on the "mountain," as the disciples did, to listen to Jesus' words in lessons such as the Sermon on the Mount (Matthew 5:1-12). For it is here, in the Beatitudes, that we are given a guide for daily living, a roadmap for the journey. Pier Giorgio modelled this behaviour for us, showing that we are all drawn to holiness and we are all called to serve.

Pier Giorgio's life certainly exemplified Christ's call to us in Matthew 25:40: "Truly I tell you, just as you did it to one of the least of these who are members of my family, you did it to me." Pier Giorgio never hesitated to share his deep spiritual life with others. He reminds us that "the faith given to me in baptism suggests to me surely; by yourself you will do nothing, but if you have God as the center of all your actions, then you will reach the goal." Pier Giorgio had the courage to tackle the mountains and the challenges of daily life by putting his faith into action. Do we have the strength to do the same?

# Reflection Questions

*I urge you with all the strength of my soul to approach the Eucharist Table as often as possible. Feed on this Bread of the Angels from which you will draw the strength to fight inner struggles... Jesus comes to me each morning in Holy Communion. I return his visit to him in the poor.*

Pier Giorgio Frassati

1. While you may not be climbing physical mountains, how can you tackle the challenges of your daily life by putting your faith into action?

2. Our actions often speak much louder than our words, and are far more effective. How do your actions reveal your faith?

3. How can you do a better job of placing God at the centre of all your actions?

# LET US PRAY +

Gracious God,

as you did for Blessed Pier Giorgio Frassati,

show us the way to you.

When we seem to have lost our way on the path,

show us the way.

When we struggle to offer ourselves to others in charity,

show us the way.

Be with us and guide us always.

We ask this through Christ our Lord.

Amen. +

# St. André Bessette

***Being a man of humility and hospitality***

*Christ has no body but yours,*
*No hands, no feet on earth but yours.*
*Yours are the eyes with which he looks*
*Compassion on this world.*

Teresa of Avila

In the life of André Bessette, we discover yet another example of God working wonders through an unlikely source. This ordinary man who never took credit for the good work he did was canonized on October 17, 2010, by Pope Benedict XVI.

Born Alfred Bessette on August 9, 1845, he was one of twelve children in a working-class Quebec family. Alfred's health was always delicate. His father, a carpenter, struggled to support his family, and was forced to take a job as a lumberman in rural Quebec. His life was cut short when he was killed in a lumbering accident. Alfred's mother, widowed at the age of 40, was left to care for her large family. Three years later, she died of tuberculosis. Alfred, an orphan at the age of twelve, was sent to live with his aunt.

His fragile health and weak constitution hampered Alfred from holding a job for long. Another obstacle was that Alfred could neither read nor write. He did, however, have a deep abiding faith and a powerful devotion to St. Joseph. Eventually, after Alfred lost job after job, his pastor, who knew of the young man's devotion and deep faith, decided to recommend him to the Congregation of the Holy Cross in Montreal. At first, the Congregation turned him down due to his poor health, but Alfred appealed to Archbishop Ignace Bourget of Montreal, who supported his request. Alfred was accepted into the order in 1872 and received the name Brother André.

Due to his lack of useful skills, his delicate health and his scant education, he was assigned the ministry of welcome as the doorkeeper of the college. He was officially admitted into the order when he made his final vows on February 2, 1874, but having no formal ministry training, he remained as doorkeeper until his death on January 6, 1937. From his place at the door of Notre Dame College, he would welcome the sick and the troubled. (Brother André often joked that when he arrived at the Order he was "shown" the door and never left!) He encouraged all who passed through these doors to pray to St. Joseph for support, and before long many people reported that their prayers had been answered.

The image of this humble man faithfully greeting all those who entered his community is powerful indeed. It reminds us of our call to be open and welcoming to all and to see the face of Christ in all we meet.

Brother André's deep devotion to St. Joseph sustained him. To honour this beloved saint, he wanted to build a chapel for St. Joseph. The idea took shape and received great support, thanks to Brother André's dedication to the project. The "chapel" eventually became St. Joseph's Oratory in Montreal. Despite huge financial roadblocks and troubles, Brother André persevered. He didn't live to see the completion of this shrine (construction began in 1924, and it was finished in 1967), but his heart is kept in a reliquary there as protection for the basilica. More than two million pilgrims visit the Oratory every year.

Brother André started small and never stopped working for God. We can hope for no greater model than this. His seemingly insignificant actions spoke volumes to those who came to know and love him. He was not a great man in the world's terms, not a brilliant theologian, and not a power broker in the Church hierarchy. He was only a humble man of unlimited faith. He would stand for hours each day, greeting strangers at the door, sharing his devotion to St. Joseph and encouraging others to share in this devotion. He always had a kind word for all who passed through his doors. His life philosophy was a humble approach to living and working and always serving – always in the persona of Christ. He was called to reflect Christ to the world to all those who crossed his threshold.

Brother André's ministry of hospitality is one we can all try to carry out: opening the doors to our worshipping communities,

welcoming the stranger, valuing the disenfranchised, and bring-
ing comfort and hope to all who enter our homes or gather in our
places of work or worship. This ministry crosses the boundaries
of race, culture, gender and level of education.

The scriptures are filled with references to welcoming the
stranger. We have already explored the story of Zacchaeus; the
Gospel of Matthew tells us, "And the king will answer them,
'Truly I tell you, just as you did it to one of the least of these who
are members of my family, you did it to me'" (25:40); and in the
Gospel of Mark Jesus says, "Whoever welcomes one such child
in my name welcomes me, and whoever welcomes me welcomes
not me but the one who sent me" (9:37). Clearly, Jesus highly
valued hospitality. Brother André heard the call to show hospitality to all he met.

Too often today, in the busyness of our lives, we lose sight of
the call to hospitality. Yet this is one of the great tools of evan-
gelization. Recent studies tell us that what Catholics want most
in their parishes is to feel welcomed and a part of their worshipping community. When we gather together as the body of Christ
to celebrate the Eucharist, we may arrive as individuals, but we
celebrate as a community. Through our baptism, we are given
the mission to spread the good news of the Gospel through our
words and our actions – not just to our family and friends, but
to all we meet. That includes making people feel welcome and
valued. Just as Brother André met and greeted pilgrims as they
arrived at his door, we are called to model hospitality and welcome at home, at work, in our community, and at church.

Brother André, through his ministry of hospitality, has been credited with thousands of miraculous cures. His spirituality was based in a deep devotion to St. Joseph and a powerful commitment to the poor and the suffering. Throughout his life, despite being revered by those who came to know and love him, Brother André never lost his humility. Though a simple, frail man who could barely read or write, he became a conduit for God's love, healing and mercy.

We are called to share in this ministry of hospitality in God's service.

## Reflection Questions

*It is with the smallest brushes that the artist paints the most exquisitely beautiful pictures.*

St. André Bessette

1. How are you a conduit of God's love?

2. Is there a strong ministry of hospitality in your parish? How can you help build and foster this sense of welcome?

3. How do you model the ministry of hospitality in your daily life?

# LET US PRAY +

Heavenly Father,
you chose Brother André
to spread devotion to St. Joseph
and to welcome and bring comfort
to the poor and the suffering.
Grant us the grace to love and serve you,
our neighbours and all those we meet.
We ask this through Christ our Lord.
Amen. +

# C.S. Lewis

## Being a prodigal son

*Faith comes from the heart as well as the mind.*

C.S. Lewis

C live Staples Lewis, the best-selling author of *The Chronicles of Narnia*, *Mere Christianity*, *The Screwtape Letters*, and *Surprised by Joy*, to name a few of his works, was not a Catholic but was a faith-filled Christian. This ordinary man who had an extraordinary talent has much to offer us for our reflection.

It is impossible in this short chapter to describe the complex faith journey that C.S. Lewis experienced. We will focus on how this man – who, as a child, was enthralled with the stories of the Bible, lost his faith and became an agnostic, and then eventually returned to his faith in a profound manner that is reflected in his writing – speaks to all of us today.

C.S. Lewis was born in Northern Ireland on November 29, 1898, the second son of Albert and Flora Lewis. Albert, a lawyer, and Flora, the daughter of a Protestant clergyman, were avid readers and practising Christians. Their home was filled with books and Lewis was encouraged to read from an early age. He developed a great love of literature, which nurtured his imagination. While he was never close to his father, he was very close to his older brother, Warren, and to his mother.

After his mother died of cancer, just before his tenth birthday, Lewis was sent to boarding school in England. He hated both the school and the teachers. This was a very difficult, unhappy time for him, since he had just lost his mother. One positive aspect of his time at the school was that he began his personal faith journey there. This was the first time he had read the Bible for himself, and he began to formulate his own religious beliefs. The fact that Jesus came to earth as a man, was crucified, died and rose again for all people, including him, became central to his life and played a significant role in much of his future writing.

As well as embracing the stories of the Bible, he turned to prayer for comfort and guidance – not the structured prayers he prayed at school or at church, but his own creations, his personal conversations with God. He understood that all conversation with God is prayer.

Lewis's journey was not to be a smooth one. He struggled with his faith during those early years. His voracious appetite for reading was both a help and a hindrance to him. He developed a fascination for Nordic myths and legends, and by the age of twelve, began to seriously question and lose his fledgling Christian faith in light of a more pluralistic view of God and creation. He also struggled with his schooling. By the time he was fifteen, his father arranged for a private tutor for him. This tutor, William Kirkpatrick, was an atheist who challenged Lewis's creative mind and introduced him to great works of literature by the likes of Homer, Dante and Molière. Lewis's struggles with his faith were fuelled by his teacher's atheism. He moved farther and farther away from the Church and from the Bible that he had loved so much.

In 1915, he was accepted at Oxford University, but left in 1917 to enter military training for the First World War. Just before his nineteenth birthday, he was sent to the front lines, where he witnessed much suffering, disease and death. He was eventually wounded and sent home; he returned to Oxford to complete his studies and in time began teaching in the English Department.

At Oxford, he became friends with another young writer, J.R.R. Tolkien, who would have a huge influence on both Lewis's writing and his life. Tolkien – later author of *The Lord of the Rings* trilogy and *The Hobbit* – was a practising Catholic who formed a literary group, the Inklings, for discussion and debates; Lewis was invited to join. It was here that Lewis began to return to his Christian faith. At the age of 31, Lewis, through his association with these Christian friends, came to realize that God was waiting for him to return to the fold. This is a good reminder that amid all the chaos, the challenges and the side journeys we take as we travel our journey of faith, God doesn't give up on us. We are the ones who leave God; he is always waiting for our return. As we read in Luke 15:7, "Just so, I tell you, there will be more joy in heaven over one sinner who repents than over ninety-nine righteous people who need no repentance."

Lewis's journey back to the Church was not an easy one; it was fraught with struggles and challenges. He called himself "the most reluctant convert in England." But return he did, and became firmly rooted in the Church of England – to the dismay of Tolkien, who had hoped that Lewis would find his spiritual home in the Catholic Church.

Lewis developed a strong belief in communal worship with one's local church. For him, there was no need to shop around for different styles of worship or forms of service. What was important was the communal encounter with God.

Lewis's great gift to us is in his writings. Throughout his work we see powerful Christian influences that call us to a deeper understanding of and relationship with God. In *The Great Divorce,* a book written in response to William Blake's *The Marriage of Heaven and Hell,* Lewis writes, "There are two kinds of people: those who say to God, Thy will be done and those to whom God says, 'All right then, have it your way.'" In *The Joyful Christian,* Lewis tells us, "Aim at heaven and you will get Earth thrown in: aim at Earth and you will get neither." This man who struggled so much in his personal faith journey has, through his great gift, brought insight and clarity to many through his writing.

Lewis is often considered a modern prophet. He thought of this earthly life as a waiting room – a place where we prepare for a greater world. He not only expressed his faith through his gift of communication, but also by devoting ten percent of his income to assist the poor and suffering during the war years.

We can't leave our discussion of C.S. Lewis without mentioning one of his greatest works: *The Lion, the Witch, and the Wardrobe.* In this work, which is the second book in the Narnia series, Lewis uses the image of a door as a metaphor for our hearts. It is through the door of the magic wardrobe that the four children in the story enter the world of Narnia. There they begin their adventures in that land, and encounter Aslan the lion, who is lord of Narnia and a Christ figure.

In all that Lewis wrote, whether for children or for adults, we find many different levels of understanding, not unlike the parables that Christ told. The lessons of the parables were always more important than the story itself. In the same way, Lewis's writing is never just about the story, but is always filled with symbolism and messages to be unpacked. On one level, *The Lion, the Witch, and the Wardrobe* is a story of right and wrong, of darkness versus light, and can easily be read on that level, but it is also filled with powerful Christian imagery where Aslan is willing to die for the sins of others and rise again – an echo of the Paschal Mystery.

"The success of a piece of literature," Lewis said, "should be gauged not by the age of its readers, but by the impact that particular book has upon the readers." I encourage you to read this wonderful writer and to ponder the images and ideas he paints for us with his rich palette of words. In C.S. Lewis we have an ordinary man who struggled with his faith – who just happened to be blessed with a genius for writing and communication. We can all benefit from his genius!

# Reflection Questions

*All our merely natural activities will be accepted if they are offered to God, even the humblest, and all of them, even the noblest, will be sinful if they are not.*

C.S. Lewis

1. C.S. Lewis's faith journey was greatly affected by those with whom he associated. How has your journey been affected, nurtured and influenced by others?

2. Use Christ's parable of the Prodigal Son found in Luke 15:11-32 to reflect on God patiently waiting for us to return when we stray.

3. C.S. Lewis was greatly influenced by strong role models in his life. Who would you identify as being a strong, faith-filled role model in your life and why?

# LET US PRAY +

Heavenly Father,
thank you for celebrating when
someone who is lost comes home.
At times, and in different ways,
we have all been lost,
and you cared enough
to celebrate our return.
While we may wander off the path,
you are always waiting for us with open arms.
Help us to always seek you when we are lost.
We ask this through Christ our Lord.
Amen. +

# Venerable Michael McGivney

## Being a leader of men

*"No one has greater love than this,*
*to lay down one's life for one's friends."*

John 15:13

This scripture from the Gospel of John exemplifies the life of Father Michael McGivney, the founder of one of the wonderful Catholic fraternal organizations, the Knights of Columbus. Before founding this amazing organization, Father McGivney was a parish priest who was actively involved in building and sustaining his faith community.

Michael McGivney was born in 1852 in Waterbury, Connecticut, the first of thirteen children, six of whom died in infancy. As a child, he experienced firsthand the struggles of a large immigrant family living in a new land. At the age of thirteen, he worked in a spoon factory in deplorable conditions. At seventeen he left home and travelled to Canada to study for the priesthood.

His studies were cut short when his father died; Michael was forced to return home. Despite the sorrow and poverty that surrounded him, he learned about the power of faith and love, and about the importance and strength of the family unit. He completed his studies a few years later and was ordained a priest in 1877.

As a young pastor, McGivney witnessed the terrible working conditions of the immigrant. Many families lost their principal breadwinner to these dangerous, low-paying jobs and faced even greater struggles as they tried to rebuild their lives. McGivney found this situation unacceptable. Something had to be done.

He decided to find a way to strengthen the religious faith of families pushed to the breaking point and to provide financial support for families overwhelmed by the death of the breadwinner.

In 1881, he founded the Knights of Columbus, an organization for Catholic men. Primarily through dues and donations, he was able to offer assistance to fatherless families. The Knights of Columbus also aimed to offer moral support and encouragement to sustain men who were living in these horrible conditions through a spiritual fraternity. McGivney saw that building communities of support would sustain and empower these men and would help to strengthen the family unit.

The organization grew quickly – clearly, the need was great. And it kept growing. Father McGivney died as a result of complications of tuberculosis at the age of 38 and thus did not see how his vision would bear much fruit. Today, the Knights of Columbus have over 1.7 million members worldwide. Councils can be found in most states of the USA, Canada, the Philippines, Mexico, and several Central American and Caribbean countries.

Father McGivney speaks to us today as a model of servant leadership. He understood the aspirations as well as the struggles, challenges and temptations faced by the men who worked to feed their families. He became known as an apostle to these men, called to lead others to a deeper relationship with Christ.

He was a mentor, a model for struggling immigrants, helping to draw them into a more caring life of service to their neighbours and community. At a time when there was much personal suffering and strife, McGivney helped a generation see that by working together with common goals, they could support each other and grow as a community. This vision lives on today, in the tremendous community work the Knights do. Their work always extends into the community to strengthen and build families.

Father McGivney challenges us to work tirelessly to grow spiritually as Catholic men and to foster a community of hospitality. As we read in the Letter to the Hebrews, "Do not neglect to show hospitality to strangers, for by doing that some have entertained angels without knowing it" (Hebrews 13:2).

Father McGivney's belief in the strength of the family led him to be fascinated by the power of being needed and by objectives being fulfilled within the family. This led him to think that these could easily be transferred to our belonging in the Church. He believed that if he could assist families in their struggles, individual families would be strengthened but also families would become more involved in the larger parish family. His concept of "strengthen the family and you strengthen the Church" certainly remains true today. While the challenges facing families have changed, their need for support continues.

Like St. André Bessette, Father Michael McGivney modelled the need for understanding a true ministry of hospitality. Through his outreach, care and concern for the impoverished and the downtrodden, he welcomed all as he would welcome Christ.

We, too, are called to model this behaviour at a time when many people are experiencing despair, violence and suffering today. The family unit that Father McGivney struggled so hard to protect and sustain needs our ongoing support and encouragement. The need to work together as a large body to protect and build family relationships is as important as it ever was.

It has been said that it is hard to be a Christian by yourself. Father McGivney knew this all too well. He helps us see, through his actions, that most of the message of Jesus comes down to how we relate to one another. Our challenge is to live with others as Christ did. Doing so today is just as difficult in our pluralistic, materialistic world as it was when Jesus first gave the apostles the message to care for those in need over 2,000 years ago.

The Knights of Columbus continue to carry on their founder's legacy – serving God, families and neighbours in countless ways. The Knights embody a firm commitment to charity, unity, fraternity and patriotism. Father McGivney's example of being always willing to listen, advise and comfort draws us to imitate his virtues within our various vocations.

## Reflection Questions

*"Do not neglect to show hospitality to strangers ...."*

(Hebrews 13:2)

1. What can you do to help make your parish and community greater places of care and concern for those in need? How can you find support and common purpose with other men?

2. How can you see yourself working within your community to help others grow closer to Christ?

3. Father McGivney worked hard to help the men of his flock understand what it means to be church. How can you be church for those you meet each day?

## LET US PRAY +

Heavenly Father,
protector of the poor,
you called your priest Michael McGivney
to be an apostle of Christian family life
and to lead others to a life of service to their neighbours.
May we follow his example
as we answer the call of your Son
to care for those in need.
We ask this through Christ our Lord.
Amen. +

# For Further Reading

## Men of the Old Testament

1. Abraham – Genesis 15–21, Genesis 22
2. David – 1 Samuel 17:1-58, 2 Samuel 11
3. Job – The Book of Job
4. Daniel – Daniel 1:1–6:28
5. Jacob – Genesis 25–27, 42, 45–49

## Men of the New Testament

6. St. Joseph – Matthew 1, Luke 1
7. Nicodemus – John 3:1-21
8. Zacchaeus – Luke 19:1-10
9. The Centurion – Matthew 8:5-13, Luke 7:1-10, Mark 15:39
10. St. Peter – Mark 1:16-18, Matthew 14:22-33, Matthew 16:13-20, John 13:1-11

## Men of the Modern Age

11. St. Thomas More – *The Last Four Things* by Thomas More; *A Man for All Seasons* by Robert Bolt (a play)
12. Blessed Pier Giorgio Frassati – *A Man of the Beatitudes*, by Luciana Frassati
13. St. André Bessette – *Brother André: A Saint for Today*, by Georges Madore; *Brother André: Friend of the Suffering, Apostle of St. Joseph*, by Jean-Guy Dubue
14. C.S. Lewis – *C.S. Lewis: A Complete Guide to His Life and Works*, by Walter Hooper
15. Venerable Michael McGivney – *Parish Priest: Michael McGivney and American Catholicism*, by Douglas Brinkley and Julie M. Fenster